THE POWER OF ANGER

TABLE OF CONTENTS

CHAPTER ONE:ANGER

We are all emotional beings irrespective of what we think or

do ,we all have those moments our emotions take control of us and we end up apologising later if we are cultured but some are too embarrassed to apologise for their tantrums.

We all get angry because of one thing or the other, some of us yell it out others keep it bolted inside and others just assume it and life goes on as if nothing happened.

Anger as a noun is defined as strong feeling of annoyance, displeasure, or hostility but as a verb it means fill (someone) with anger; provoke anger in.

In psychology anger defined as an emotion characterised by antagonism toward someone or something you feel has deliberately done you wrong.

Anger is one of the basic human emotions, as elemental as happiness, sadness, anxiety, or disgust. These emotions are tied to basic survival and were honed over the course of human history. Anger is related to the "fight, flight, or freeze" response of the sympathetic nervous system; it prepares humans to fight. But fighting doesn't necessarily mean throwing punches; it might motivate communities to combat injustice by changing laws or enforcing new behavioral norms.

Of course, anger too easily or frequently mobilized can undermine relationships and it can be deleterious to bodies in the long term. Prolonged release of the stress hormones that accompany anger can destroy neurons in areas of the brain associated with judgment and short-term memory, and weaken the immune system.

Everyone knows the feeling. It's that rage that rises when a driver is cut off on the highway—and just wants to floor it and flip the bird. Anger doesn't dissipate just because it is unleashed; in fact, that can reinforce and deepen it.

Like all emotions, anger should be monitored via self-awareness, lest it cause self-harm or erupt into hostile, aggressive, or even violent behavior toward others. Support groups for anger management are available in many cities. In group or individual settings, cognitive restructuring may be helpful, as it coaches patients on reframing unhealthy, inflammatory thoughts.

Everyone experiences anger at some point. It becomes problematic, however, when the frequency or severity of anger interferes with relationships, work performance, legal standing, or mental health. While there is no official "anger disorder," dysfunctional anger can be a symptom of manic episodes, Borderline Personality Disorder, and Intermittent Explosive Disorder. Anger doesn't require a formal diagnosis to be disruptive, or to benefit from help with its management.

Anger can be a good thing. It can give you a way to express negative feelings, for example, or motivate you to find solutions to problems. Spiritually anger is anger can be viewed at as an injustice.. Anger helps us see what is wrong and can motivate action to create positive change in the our lives.

This sort of response creates a blessing rather than a curse. But anger can also reflect and intensify our wounds and separation.
We all respond to anger differently but however we respond to it ,dedicates our future relationships with those who made us angry.
Anger can be used positively for instance,,you get fired from your job ,you get pissed off that you start your own company to become an employer

and this brings financial freedom to you and success.

Anger can be negatively used too, for instance, you get divorced by your spouse, who ends up bankrupting you in the process and leaving you in an emotional wreckage and financial comatose, you can choose to get on with your life positively but also allow life to hammer you and get angry at everyone as you find solace in the bottle and hard drugs ending up in a ditch dead .

Life in general is determined by how we respond to emotions above all how we control our anger ,as anger has the power to make or brake us .

Studies show that the ability to identify and label emotions correctly, and talk about them straightforwardly to the point of feeling understood, makes negative feelings dissipate. And the physiologic arousal that accompanies those feelings also diminishes dramatically.

But when anger is deemed unacceptable, people stay in a state of arousal, unable to pay attention to what is going on in the world around them, unable to regulate their own behavior and focused only on their inner emotional state. In fact, they tend to experience excessive physiologic arousal in situations involving negative emotions—but they tend not to display any external signs of emotional response. Imagine how that can confuse a friend or a spouse! That's because they hide their emotions but feel anxious in emotionally evocative situations.

Sometimes, however, telling someone we are angry brings feelings of relief, especially when we also express why we are angry. Psychologists believe that the relief we feel under those circumstances results not from venting the anger but from identifying the anger-arousing circumstances and working towards a solution. And that points to the positive value that anger has. It's a great motivator for change. It encourages us to speak up about something bothering us.

But it's all in how we do it, because in goading us to action about things that upset us, anger can also prompt us to overreact. So first and foremost, lengthen your fuse so that you are not reacting to every tiny upset and you can think your way to a constructive solution.

Take three deep breaths.
When you are angry, your body becomes tense. Breathing deeply will ease the tension and help lower your internal anger meter.

Change your environment.
The quickest way to uncouple yourself from an ongoing source of anger is to take a five-minute walk to get some fresh air. Stuck in traffic? Take a mental escape by turning up the radio and singing at the top of your lungs.

Know why you feel angry.
Track down the clues about the kinds of things, situation, people and events that trigger your anger. Anger often masks our deepest fears. In an angry-making situation, ask yourself what deep fears it might be stirring in you.

Let go of what is beyond your control.
You can change only yourself and your responses to others, not what others do to you. Getting angry doesn't fix the situation and makes you feel worse. If someone constantly arouses your anger, focus on the troublesome situation and brainstorm solutions.

Express yourself.
Be sure to think first and use measured tones and words that are not emotionally loaded. In a nonconfrontational way state that you are angry and identify the situation that makes you angry and why it ticks you off.

Be cautious.
There are situations in which expressing your anger holds danger. Having a jealous or abusive partner is one. Vent to a friend instead of the person who wronged you; you may wind up with some solutions you never imagined.

Be assertive, not aggressive, in expressing yourself.
Assertiveness requires speaking in an effective, nonviolent way towards a constructive goal. It may help if you rehearse your response before delivering it.

Make positive statements.
Memorize a few positive statements to say to yourself when your anger is triggered. They will remind you that you can choose your behavior instead of reacting in a knee-jerk way. For example, you might say: "I can take care of my

own needs" or "His needs are just as important as mine" or "I am able to make good choices."

We are going to discuss anger in different perspectives in the following chapters.

CHAPTER TWO:CONS OF ANGER

There are many instances we have been too angry at something or someone that we did something that we ended up regretting latter .

Take for instance your spouse cheats on you ,you find her or him in bed cheating ,some choose to walk away but in this instance you don't, you decide to get "justice " and you murder them both ,your anger is justified but not your actions, from then on you are arrested for murder and get a life sentence or get executed after a long tiring legal process .

If you had decided to walk away and seek divorce later, you wouldn't have been arrested nor executed nor caused your loved ones pain both emotionally and financially because they had to pay a lawyer to give you a fair chance at justice as they go broke.

Although your anger does have its upside, the downside of anger far outweighs any positive benefits. Besides being emotionally distressing and making you a prime candidate for a black eye, your anger can give you other things to worry about.

Anger can make you sick

When you're angry, your body reacts much the same way it does when you are experiencing any other stress reaction. Your anger triggers your body to take a defensive stance, readying yourself for any danger that may come your way. When your anger is intense and frequent, the physiological effects can be harmful. Your health is at risk, and any or all of those nasty stress-related illnesses and disorders can become linked to excessive anger.

Anger can break your heart

Recent research now indicates that your heart (or more accurately, your cardiovascular system) is particularly vulnerable to your anger and its negative effects. In his book, Anger Kills, published by Harper Perennial, Duke University researcher Redford Williams describes a number of possible ways hostility can negatively affect your cardiovascular system.

Society is full of examples of people who couldn't control their anger and ended up being more broken than before and messing up their lives just because of an emotional situation that got the better of them .

Let me use a more familiar example ,American RnB artist Chris Brown was in a romantic relationship with music sensual Rihanna and the two got into an argument,Chris ended up beating Rihanna, this led to a public outcry and Chris was prosecuted for his alleged buttery and also lost millions in promotions and endorsements deals ,he took anger management classes .

Another celebrity who had anger issues is boxing legend Mike Tyson fondly known as Iron Mike ,his anger issues led him to loose more than just his flourishing boxing career but also his finances were adversely affected due to legal suits compensations

which run into millions and no companies want to be associated with such guys .
One needs to be emotionally strong and intelligent to be able to control their anger.Emotional intelligence is something we all don't possess especially if our emotions always takes over .
Emotional intelligence is understood as the capacity to be aware of, control, and express one's emotions, and to handle interpersonal relationships judiciously and empathetically.
How many of us that can be a hundred percent sure that their emotions doesn't get the better of them once in a while?.The main deal is not to let anger be the driving force that leads you to your ruin .

CHAPTER THREE:PROS OF ANGER

Anger has a positive perspective, if you are a pessimist you will definitely angry with me on this ,because of the believe that there is always a better day coming however tougher and unforeseeable the future maybe at your current position or situation.

Anger can be a highly distressing emotion that results in all kinds of negative consequences. Yet, among the other possible stress emotions (upset, depression, grief, anxiety, and so on), anger remains the most popular and the most common. And not without reason. Anger has some appeal:

Anger is activating and mobilizing. When you're angry, you feel as if you're doing something about what's triggering your stress. You feel there is a response you can make, a way of expending energy toward resolving the distressing situation.

It can get you to take action and do something about the problem.

Anger makes you feel powerful. Anger can make you feel like you're in charge, even when you aren't. When you tell someone off or give them a tongue-lashing, you feel stronger and in control. Anger enables you to express yourself in a forceful way.

Anger often gets results. By becoming angry, as opposed to remaining calm and pleasant, you may get what you want. Many people are intimidated by anger and are more obliging when confronted with it than they normally would be.

Anger is often a respected response. We often interpret anger as standing up for ourselves and not letting others take advantage of us. And other people may see it the same way. Our anger may be labeled as assertive, strong, and confident.

For instance you get fired for your work, you get soo angry to form your own company, let's take the instance of Chinese billionaire and Alibaba/Ali

express founder Jack Ma ,who was denied admission into Harvard, couldn't get a job at KFC but went ahead to start a billion dollar company. We have many instances of guys who used anger positively and become better persons take for instance a guy who gets ditched by his fiancé, the guy decides to go back to school, gets a second degree which enables him to be promoted at work with translated
into better pay and financial freedom, gets to join the gym to vent out his anger at the training instruments this gives him a healthy body and enables him to meet more people in the long run he becomes a better person than he was earlier. We should learn to use our anger to make us better, use it as a motivation to be better and be successful as they say there is no better revenge than to be successful and happy .

Anger is a good thing if used and exploited wisely, look around your environment there are a lot of examples of people who used anger as a motivation to be better and do better, be like them don't ever let anger be your downfall buddies .

CHAPTER FOUR :EMOTIONS V/S REALITY

As much as I am encouraging you to control your anger and use it as a motivation to be better persons ,we have to face the reality that our emotions sometimes take over us ,however much we prepare ourselves .

Reality is understood as the state of things as they actually exist, as opposed to an idealistic or notional idea of them.Now you understand why it's human to get angry and sometimes to be driven by it to do things that you cannot explain once you get back to your senses .

Accepting reality means accepting yourself as you are ,with all your awesomeness and un-awesomeness ,as you try to better yourself you have to accept that you won't be perfect but focus on the better side of the equation at least you trying to be a better person than you were ,you taking responsibility and control of your life and that matters a lot than anything.

Emotions are understood as a strong feeling deriving from one's circumstances, mood, or relationships with others.We can't run away from emotions nor control then a hundred percent no matter how much we try because as being human in essence means we are emotional beings . Emotions drive us into success or failure, that's the reality of this world. One has to have passion for his or her career to be successful and vice versa ,passion is an emotion that's strong and barely controllable.

You might think that a bad mood is tied to an event that impacted you negatively, but that's not necessarily the case. Understanding that your mood is often independent of your circumstances can help you avoid making bad decisions.

We've all been told at one point or another to trust our gut, Dr. Amy Johnson at Tiny Buddha warns against letting your gut guide you down the wrong path.

You see, you are always feeling your thinking. You are not necessarily always feeling "the truth," or even your own personal truth.

Every emotion, feeling, or mood you experience follows directly from the thinking you are experiencing. That thinking is not always accurate or important. It does not always indicate what's best for you.

In reality, your feelings are nothing more than feedback about your thinking.

Feelings are not feedback about your mental health, the state of your life, or whether you have the "right" job, partner, or dietary habits. Before coming to this realization, Amy would try to change things in her life that she decided were causing her bad moods, creating a feedback loop that kept her from seeing clearly. For example, she'd notice that she was in a bad mood occasionally at her job, and so she started to only see the negative aspects of her work, and then decided she would only be happy if she found a new one.

In reality, her bad mood was just a random symptom of some negative thoughts. They happen, and we can't really control them. In fact, dwelling on the bad mood, and trying to change the things that caused it, will only serve to make it worse.

As it turns out, much of the negative experience of emotions is the cover-up. It's when you resist, hide, or try to change those emotions that you experience them as painful.

When you do that, you're playing with mental superglue again. You're putting so much pressure and focus on those emotions that they are held in place. Remember, when you don't hold on to thought and emotion, new thought and emotion rushes in.

The big takeaway here is to ride out the storm when you get in a bad mood, and try not to tie it to anyone or anything without sleeping on it first. If it keeps reoccurring, it might be time to think about making some life changes, but it's dangerously easy to make that determination prematurely.

Reality has always been in conflict with emotions for instance, you have a crush on someone, let's say a celebrity ,that's emotional and happens to the best of us ,but reality is you have fewer chances of being in that relationship with that celebrity more than just being a normal fan of hers or his but the reality doesn't stop your emotions about her or him .

Now it's better to understand that there is nothing wrong with being emotional over thing but the problem is when you become obsessed over things or anyone .An obsession is understood as an idea or thought that continually preoccupies or intrudes on a person's mind.

An obsession can be compared to an addiction, and all addictions have more negative impacts on one's life than positive ones hence they should be avoided at all costs .

Reality is we all get obsessed with something or someone once in a while because this is life and to err is human, but that isn't a pass to let our emotions control our lives or take us to the drainage .

CHAPTER FIVE:CONCLUSION

In conclusion,we should all try our best to control our anger and if all seems impossible we should seek help from professionals.

Dr. Larisa Wainer opinionated that , Like other emotions, anger is a normal, healthy human feeling that is neither good nor bad and in fact, has adaptive properties. Anger helps us handle emergency situations by providing a quick burst of energy and strength, so we can react to threats of danger. Anger pushes us to reach goals by creating motivation through frustration. In relationships, anger encourages us to address outstanding issues, which facilitates intimacy and growth. When not managed properly, anger can cause serious damage. Unresolved, recurrent anger can lead to health problems (hypertension, cardiovascular disease), interpersonal issues (damaged/terminated relationships, problems at work, isolation), decreased life satisfaction, and physical and emotional harm to self and others. Why is anger so overpowering and compelling? Our brains are actually wired to get us to act before we can properly consider the consequences of our actions! The emotion center of the brain, the amygdale, responsible for alarming us to possible threats gets us reacting before the prefrontal cortex, responsible for rational thinking, is able to check if our reaction is reasonable. The hormonal arousal from anger can last many hours and even days, leaving us vulnerable to ongoing irritation and new angry episodes. In addition, anger brings secondary gain. It helps release pent up stress, acts as a shield by covering up painful emotions (i.e. fear, loss, guilt, shame), gets attention, pushes people to act, and feels righteous. Though it's tough to disengage it, indulging in anger leads to more anger, leaves others defensive and distant, and sets up possible harm – emotional, physical or both, creating a cycle of defensiveness and resentment that's hard to break.

Managing anger properly is not an instinct, but a skill that has to be learned. The good news is that bad anger habits can be un- learned, with proper self-understanding, monitoring and behavioral change. If you'd like to change how you manage your anger, it's important to increase your personal anger awareness. You will need to become your own investigator. First, see if you can learn your personal "early warning" signs. These could include body sensations: heart rate increase, tightness in your jaw, shallow breathing, a wrinkle in your brow, closing fists, headache or stomach ache, forming early on in the process. You can also look for early stage angry feelings, like annoyance or irritation.

Interrupting anger in its early stages is exponentially easier than when your frustration has grown into ballistic rage.

Situations that set us off tend to repeat, and it's helpful to keep track of them in an effort to identify your recurring personal anger triggers. Do you get angry when your needs aren't being met? Basic needs could be: tired, hungry, hot/cold, or sick. For example, you might notice that you are getting into arguments when you skip a meal or in the evening, before bed, when you are tired. Emotional needs might include: feeling rushed or overwhelmed, lack of attention or being heard, experiencing loss, loneliness, not feeling loved. An example would be losing control of anger when you are in a rush to get to work or right before a separation through travel or when your partner seems to need alone time. Perhaps you are triggered when your expectations are unmet (i.e. people running late, driving slowly, not responding to your outreach) or when you feel "out of control" (i.e. overwhelmed with responsibilities, not in charge of a task, ignored/superseded in terms of your needs). Maybe your triggers include being treated unjustly or threatened in some way? Make a mental or written note about your specific recurring patterns.

Take a moment to reflect on where some of your anger patterns may come from. Since anger management is learned, consider some of your role models, for better or for worse. How did the significant people in your life manage anger? Are there any anger habits that you may have picked up? Do any of your fights resemble those that you've witnessed? Perhaps your parents argued about money or leaving the house late. Do these same themes set you off? Next time you get angry in a way that feels familiar, try to reflect on any triggers or grudges from the long- ago past that may have followed you into the present.

Finally take a look at your cognition. If the thoughts swirling in your mind are focused on: feeling threatened, not getting your way, predicting the negative, seeking revenge or blaming, the more you engage them, the more fuel you will provide your anger to grow.

Interpretation plays an important role as well. When we are angry, we typically make an assessment involving three components: 1) that we are being harmed or victimized, 2) that this situation or person is causing us harm deliberately, and 3) that the provoking situation or person is wrong to harm us and should behave differently. The problem with these trigger thoughts is that they are often inaccurate. Since sociopaths make up a miniscule percentage of the population, take solace in the fact that most people act the way they act for a variety of complicated personal reasons, some of which are not under their conscious control. Most people are truly doing their best based on their needs, fears, prior history, what they know and what they don't know. If they are stuck, do you have to be, too?.